From Liz on
Father's Day
1999

IMAGES of America

PEACH COUNTY

THE WORLD'S PEACH PARADISE

A Song of the Georgia Peach

Born of the sun and nourishing rain,
   Union of dew and glow;
Flushed with the pride of a hundred dawns,
   Cooled by the green below;
Sweetened by smiles of the Summer noon,
   Hanging just out of reach—
The loveliest, lusciousest fruit on earth—
   The beautiful Georgia Peach!

Take from me apples of cider fresh,
   Rob me of plum and pear;
Lose every orange of juicy gold,
   Let not a vinyard bear;
Apricot's rose from its cheek may fade,
   Melons may dry and bleach,
If thick in the low green orchard hangs
   That beautiful Georgia Peach.

IMAGES of America

PEACH COUNTY
THE WORLD'S PEACH PARADISE

Marilyn Neisler Windham

ARCADIA

First published 1997
Copyright © Marilyn Neisler Windham, 1997

ISBN 0-7524-0549-7

Published by Arcadia Publishing,
an imprint of the Chalford Publishing Corporation
One Washington Center, Dover, New Hampshire 03820
Printed in Great Britain

Library of Congress Cataloging-in-Publication Data applied for

Contents

Introduction		7
Acknowledgments		8
1.	The World's Peach Paradise	9
2.	The Sun Goddess: 1922	35
3.	Georgia's Crowning Beauty: 1923	45
4.	Peach of the World: 1924	61
5.	The Trail of Pink Pedals: 1925	85
6.	The Prodigal Peach: 1926	105
Afterword		127

The peach pickers in one of the many peach orchards of the J.H. Hale farm worked from sunrise to sunset. The popular peach of the time was the Elberta peach.

The legislative bill that created Peach County out of parts of Macon and Houston Counties was signed in 1924. Peach was the last county in Georgia to be formed. From left to right are: Emmett Houser, lawyer and Georgia legislator who wrote the bill creating the county; Charles H. Jackson of Byron, Georgia, legislator; H.C. Neil, mayor of Fort Valley; and Joe E. Davidson, Georgia legislator who presented the bill. Seated is Governor Thomas W. Hardwick.

Introduction

Located in Georgia's heartland, Peach County emerged from Macon and Houston Counties in 1924 to honor the largest and most popular agricultural crop of the time. The story of this area began with the Creek Indians. However, in the early 1800s, whites from North and South Carolina began settlement west of the Ocmulgee River. It was in what is now the town of Fort Valley that James Abbington Everett (1788–1849), a North Carolina native, came to seek his fortune.

As early as 1825 Everett built a trading post at the junction of two Native American trails. He named the place Fort Valley after his contemporary, Arthur Fort. Fort was a legislator from nearby Milledgeville who had served in the Revolutionary War.

Everett gained much wealth from his marriage into the Creek Nation. His first wife, Cuseena, was the daughter of Timpoochie Barnard, one of the leaders of the Creeks and signer of the 1821 Treaty of Indian Springs.

Everett contributed much to the growth of the area by donating land and money for the building of the first school and church in Fort Valley. His greatest success was convincing the Southwestern Railroad Company to run their line through town. Although Everett did not live to see the first train arrive in 1852, his legacy became monumental when, in the 1880s, the peach industry as we know it came into being.

All through the nineteenth century there were peaches planted in the area. In 1884, on his Willow Lake Plantation, located south of Fort Valley, near Marshallville, Samuel Henry Rumph was busy developing one of the most popular peach varieties of all time. It was the Elberta peach, named after his wife. Rumph also developed ways to ship the perishable fruit up north with refrigerated train cars. These developments would change peach farming into a multi-million dollar industry.

By 1921, one third of the peaches shipped from Georgia came from Fort Valley. Millions of peach trees had been planted, and business was booming. There were as many as fourteen passenger trains stopping in the small town of three thousand people. Hotels were springing up. There was an opera house, bowling alley, Chinese laundry, two movie theaters, a pressing club, and many other various stores. There were peach inspectors, brokers, and all sorts of people arriving in town connected to the industry. Already the area had been proclaimed a "Peach Paradise."

The great enthusiasm for the peach was taken one step further in 1922, when a young local woman, Miss Etta Carithers, came up with the idea of a peach blossom festival. It would be an annual event, held when the peaches were in full bloom. The world would be invited to see how well the peach industry had done. Also, the citizens of the north end of Houston county desired a county of their own, to be called Peach. What a wonderful way to convince the people of Georgia that Fort Valley and Byron deserved that honor.

There were five festivals, 1922–1926. The little town of Fort Valley outdid itself every year until forty thousand people were attending from all over the world. There were barbecues, parades, and pageants. It was as if a fairy tale was being played out in nearby fields and orchards. Hollywood, in the form of movie studios, came to film the affairs. *National Geographic* even recorded the 1925 festival in one of its issues. Compared with Mardi Gras and California's Rose Festival, the Peach Blossom Festivals were beyond comprehension in creativity and imagination. The small rural place had now become the "World's Peach Paradise."

Acknowledgments

With the publication of this book, a longtime dream has become a reality. For many years, the events of the Fort Valley Peach Blossom Festivals have drawn me back in time to that magical period of the 1920s. It, to me, was a story that had to be told.

I would like to thank the staff of the Peach Public Libraries for their generous help and the gracious sharing of their local history collection. Also, it is fitting that I recognize Beth Forrester, Gilda Stanberry-Cotney, and Dottie Wright for their untiring assistance in this project. For other contributions of pictures or collaboration of information, I thank Wilton Walton, Mrs. May Davidson, Mrs. Mildred Mathews, and Mrs. Carolyn Ruffo.

I could not have completed this work without them.

One
The World's Peach Paradise

This photograph was taken in Fort Valley, facing southeast down Main Street toward the J.F. Troutman house. Note the various architectural styles of the buildings and how wide the street was. The Troutman house was moved to that lot between 1906 and 1920. The house was built prior to the Civil War, about a mile south of its present location. The town of Fort Valley was incorporated in 1856.

The picture shows an overview of the north middle section of Main Street. In the foreground was the office of the local paper, *The Leader Tribune*. Fort Valley had maintained a newspaper

since before 1859. Note the dry goods store next door with a sampling of its wares out front.

North Railroad Street ran parallel to the railroad toward the Coca Cola bottling plant. On the left was Samuel M. Halprin's dry goods store. Mr. Halprin immigrated to this country in 1900 from Riga, Latvia. Next door to Halprin's store was the New Dixie Hotel. Rooms were always in demand because of the many inspectors and brokers who came to town during peach season.

This photograph shows a view looking in the opposite direction on North Railroad Street. The Winona Hotel stands in the background. Along the street, men were laying pipes for the water system. On the right was the American Sanitary Lunchroom. Note the wagons on the street.

On Church Street, emerging from the residential area into town, was the water tower. It was taken down and moved in 1926. The tank itself was 18 feet in diameter and 25 feet in depth. On the left was a series of stores, beginning with a furniture store.

Looking down Church Street in the opposite direction was the Coca Cola bottling plant, located on the right. In the background was the water tower and in the foreground was one of the three hotels in town. This business was then known as the S.H. Bassett Rooming House.

This group of men often met at the Postell Boarding House located downtown. Misses Julia and Lou Postell ran the business, which they inherited from their father. Sometimes there were special events held at the boarding house. In 1921, there was "The Bug House Banquet" which

was given in honor of Jiggs, Maggie, and Dinty (popular comic strip characters). The program consisted of many toasts, a song or two, and several stories. Not to be excluded, Miss Lou Postell recited "Little Bo Peep."

The Winona Hotel was originally called the Harris House. Built in 1883 by H.C. Harris, it had fifty gas-lit rooms. The outside porches were removed and the name changed in 1918. Since it was located across from the railroad, it was a very popular place.

The Evans Building was built around 1910. It first housed the Citizen Bank. On the second floor were offices of various lawyers and doctors. On the third floor were two large rooms used for entertainment and meeting purposes.

The Georgia Agricultural Works Building sat at the corner of Anderson Avenue and Church Street for many years. The business was started in the latter part of the 1800s. Cotton gins and farming implements were the main products.

The Wright Building sat on the south side of Main Street. It housed offices of mostly lawyers on the second floor. The Exchange Bank was on the first. Several banks had already been established in Fort Valley. Others were Dow-Law, First National, Citizens Bank, and Bank of Fort Valley.

The railroad had been one of the most vital players in the growing life of Fort Valley. Pictured are two of the railroad buildings.

The Union Passenger Station was kept quite busy with as many as fourteen passenger trains stopping daily.

The First Baptist Church was established in 1852, with seven founding members. The wooden structure was built in 1856 but burned in 1935. It was replaced with a brick building on the same site at the corner of Miller and College Streets.

The Fort Valley United Methodist Church was the first church established in Fort Valley. It was organized in 1840 as the Old Pond Church. In 1847, the church moved closer to the center of town. In 1901, the congregation built the present brick structure, at the corner of Church and Miller Streets. The annex was then added in 1918. The church is noted for its beautiful stained-glass windows.

In 1866, the first free black church was established in Fort Valley. It eventually was named Ushers Temple C.M.E. Church. The first building burned in 1891 and was rebuilt in 1895 under the leadership of Rev. Lee O'Neal. In 1958, fire again destroyed the church, but a new building was later constructed on the same site. From Usher's Temple came several others churches in the community. The members of the church were very supportive in helping to create the first free black school, called Fort Valley High and Industrial School.

Fort Valley High and Industrial School was established in 1895 for the education of blacks. In 1939, the school became Fort Valley State College. The school's emphasis was on agriculture and trades related to farming. For many years the school held "ham and egg" shows. They were competitions where farmers showed their eggs, hams, and other farm products for awards. The shows were started by Otis O'Neal in an effort to teach black farmers the right way to preserve their produce.

Fort Valley State College Chapel is shown in the above photograph. The college has been associated with the Episcopal Church since shortly after its beginning as Fort Valley High and Industrial School.

With a strong educational system already established for blacks, a new camp for black youths was built 7 miles south of Fort Valley in 1939. It was known as Camp John Hope and provided recreational activities for black children age ten years and older. The camp was located on 222 acres. It had a large pond, cabins, and athletic fields, as well as meeting facilities.

The first public school for whites in Fort Valley was built in the 1880s and was called Grady Institute. In 1912, a new school was built down the street on Everett Square. The building was designed by Phil Scroggs, son of the principal of Grady Institute. The new school had grades one through eleven. The Everett Square structure remained until the early 1950s, when it was torn down and a smaller building was constructed.

Fort Valley High School, built in 1927, provided much needed additional space.

One of the oldest streets in Fort Valley is College Street. It was named for all the schools that were built along the avenue. Included were the first boy's school built in the 1830s, a female seminary built in the 1850s, and finally Grady Institute, built in the 1880s. Many of the homes constructed in the late 1800s and early 1900s still remain. The second house on the left was built by Samuel Rumph, founder of the peach industry. He built the home in 1894 for his mother, Caroline.

Anderson Avenue was another early residential street in Fort Valley. It was named for Brigadier General Charles D. Anderson, a popular local Confederate soldier. Many of the older houses on this street have since been torn down.

The Henry C. Harris house was one of the most elegant houses in Fort Valley. It sat on the corner of Beauty Square, now known as Everett Square. Beauty Square was so named because of

all the beautiful girls that lived in the homes surrounding the area.

The Colonial Revival-style house was built by George Harris around 1913. It was for many years the home of Miss Helen Marshall. The property was part of the Grady Institute school until 1912. The house sits on the corner of Miller Street and Central Avenue.

W.C. Wright built this house for his family in 1922. It is of the Italian Renaissance style. Wright was a pharmacist-turned-banker who died before he could occupy the house. The house sits at the corner of Miller and West Church Streets. The house later became the home of the Fort Valley Woman's Club.

Albert James Evans (1875–1949) was considered a pioneer peach grower. He became one of the most influential men in the peach business and eventually was called "The Peach King." Being the great business man that he was, Evans was able to set the price of peaches up and down the Atlantic seaboard. When thinking of peaches in the first half of the twentieth century, one had to think about A.J. Evans.

Moss Lake Farm near FORT VALLEY, Ga.

There were many farming operations around the town. Not all had peaches, and many had a diversity of crops. Moss Lake Farm was one of the numerous farms that harvested cotton. Other

crops planted in the area were cantaloupes, watermelons, corn, asparagus, and pecans.

West of town was Hale Georgia Orchards. Hale's Packing House was one of the busiest places to be during the summer months. J.H. Hale, of South Glastonbury, Connecticut, had purchased 2,000 acres of peach orchards at the turn of the century. He also had 900 acres planted in fruit in New England.

The peach packers were gathered together for this photograph. They worked long hours in hot sheds. It was imperative to get the peaches on the train as quickly as possible so they would not perish or get too soft.

Many of the larger peach growers had their own railroad spur to their packing shed so that their peaches could get to market faster and in good shape. Some of the smaller orchards had to haul their peaches by wagon or truck. Above is the Albaugh's Packing House.

Samuel Rumph developed the system for hauling peaches in refrigerated train cars to market. Inside the cars were racks that held the ice so that the peaches would remain firm and keep their color until they reached the stores.

Inside the packing shed, mostly women worked grading the peaches. J.H. Hale was known as "Red-Label Hale." Hale found that many Northern growers put their best fruit on top of the box and then packed culls underneath to fool the buyer. Hale used the slogan, "You see the top, you

see it all." He put red labels on boxes that held the best selected fruit. White labels represented second-grade peaches and blue labels represented third grade. What you saw on the label was what you got throughout the entire box.

In 1925, the Atlantic Ice and Coal Company built a new million dollar plant in Fort Valley. This addition was very useful to the peach growers, who used the ice for shipping purposes. The first year, the plant sold 50,000 tons of ice to cool 17,200 railroad cars filled with peaches.

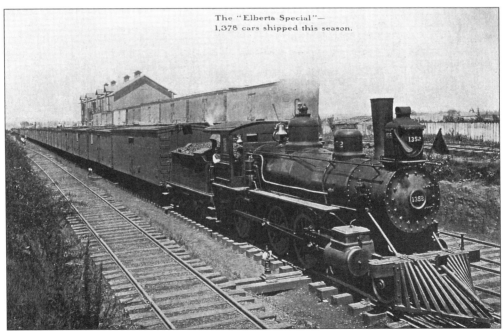

This train was called the "Elberta Special," after Samuel Rumph's greatest peach, the Elberta. It was one of many that hauled peaches from central Georgia to Northern markets.

Two
The Sun Goddess: 1922

In a quote about the first Peach Blossom Festival, the idea and spirit of the event were conveyed by an unknown writer who wrote, "Out of the magic created by countless peach trees in full bloom and out of the spirit of a city that handles more peaches than any other in the world, grew the great Peach Blossom Festival held in Fort Valley, Georgia, on March 14, 1922."

A true American festival, the celebration had the distinction of being one of the few big folk carnivals that sprung spontaneously from the people of America. Mardi Gras, in Louisiana, is a heritage of France. The Rose Carnival of California is of Spanish origin. But the Peach Blossom Festival was all-American.

So successful was the first carnival heralding the spring appearance of the Peach Blossoms that it became a permanent institution, to be held as long as there were peach blooms... With the blooms upon their branches, the trees make the whole country a pink paradise in springtime. Not Holland with its tulips and not Japan with its cherry blossoms can be compared to that magic peach country in the spring.

The poetry and romance of this wonderful land of blooms and the charm of the entire peach industry itself made up the spiritual background of the first festival. The great fete truly typified the poetry of the blossoms and the wonder of the industry."

So the first festival was born with its royalty, free barbecue, rides through the blooming orchards, speeches by the governor and other prominent Georgians, and finally the wonderful pageant called *The Sun Goddess*. The pageant brought a certain cultural intrigue to the event. Over two hundred local people acted out the Japanese masque. Actors played out the story amid the peach trees; there the king and queen were crowned, and the royal court paraded before those in attendance. Over ten thousand people attended the first festival. It was said that the barbecue was the largest ever held in Georgia. Twelve thousand pounds of meat were prepared. Over 350 gallons of Brunswick stew, 500 gallons of coffee, 3,000 loaves of bread, and 3 barrels of pickles were served that day. The festival was declared a great success. The whole town had come together to show the world the peach industry, and the world had come. This initial success was the springboard for making it an annual festival.

The king and queen of Fort Valley's first Peach Blossom Festival were Dr. A.J. Titus and Miss Thelma Wilson (pictured above). The candidates for the honor had to be at least seventeen years of age and were voted on by residents of the Ninth District of Houston County. Dr. Titus was actually a stand-in for the king of the festival. R.S. Braswell was elected to the position but had to decline due to illness. The king's costume was made of white satin and gold. His robe was purple velvet and ermine. The queen's gown was made from Parisian satin and lace. She too wore a purple robe with ermine. It was noted that she was also adorned with family-owned jewels which were "costly and rare."

The king, queen, and their court paraded through the peach orchard. The heralds with their trumpets proclaimed the coming of the royalty. The trumpeters were Henry Mathews and Joseph Kinney. The flower girls were Martha Gray Carithers, Sara Martin, Ruth Howard McMillan, and Gladys Soloman.

Miss Lucy Finney was the designer of all of the costumes used for the pageant. The women of Fort Valley then made all the outfits. For every detail of the festival, there was a committee formed to see that each task was completed with excellence. The organization of the event worked, for there were no problems reported.

A group of ladies was assigned to give out tags for the visitors to wear. The tags were designed to look like a peach. From left to right are: (front row) Miss Lucile Cox, Miss Mildred Anderson, Miss Louis DuPree, Miss Louis Campbell, Miss Margaret Branham, and Miss Dorothy DuPree; (back row) Miss Juanita Rawlings, Miss Frances Engston, Miss Emily Braswell, Miss Ruby Duke, and Miss Mildred Jones.

In this portrait are a few of the many local residents who took part in the festival. From left to right are: (front row) Miss Margaret Whiting, Miss Doris Mathews, A.J. Evans ("The Peach King"), Miss Juanita Rawlings, and Miss Lucile Cox; (back row) Miss Mildred Anderson, Miss Annie Andrey Fagan, Miss Mildred Mathews, and Miss Viloula White.

The top picture shows members of the cast of the masque, *The Sun Goddess*. The middle picture is photograph of the ten thousand people who came to see this pink, blossoming fairyland.

The bottom picture shows the crowd being fed at the barbecue. Everything at the festival was free of charge.

The barbecue pits were 510 feet long and one hundred men supervised the cooking. One hundred and fifteen hogs, seven yearlings, and three "fat" hens were barbecued for the festival. The cooking began on Sunday at midnight and ended on Tuesday at midnight. The tables used to serve all the food, end to end, extended over a mile.

The men in charge of the food worked long and hard to have everything prepared in time. Just how they estimated and then fed the large crowd that attended was a great feat in itself. On the left is B.J. Champion, committee chairman of the drinks for the barbecue. Lemonade and coffee were served. On the right is J.L. Everett, the man considered the "Georgia Barbecue King" for all the barbecues he supervised. He was the grandson of James Abbington Everett, who founded Fort Valley.

As many children as possible were used in the pageant. In *The Sun Goddess*, the little actors played the part of villagers. In the course of the story they tried to convince the Sun Goddess not to leave the world, for her light was needed by all.

The nymphs of the woodland danced to restore the favor of the Sun Goddess. She became angry at the villagers for ignoring her and had retreated to a cave. In an effort to lure her out of the darkness, rice maidens, cherry blossom maidens, wisteria maidens, and the Goddess of the Orchard danced and made bids for her to return. Their efforts were to no avail. It was only when the Sun Goddess saw her own beauty in a mirror did she agree to come out and shine once again. The play ended with the line: "Goddess or mortal, all women are vain." In the tree on the left was Miss Dorothy DuPree, who played the Soul-of-the-Butterflies.

Two of the star female roles in the masque were played by Miss Etta Carithers, as the Goddess of the Orchard, and Miss Emily Braswell, as the Sun Goddess. Miss Carithers was credited with having been the originator of the Peach Blossom Festival concept. She was, at the time, director of the Fort Valley Community Services program. Community Services organizations were set up all over the country from funds left over from World War I. Their purpose was to help towns provide recreational and cultural activities for the community. Out of the cultural interest came not only the festival but also a community band, classes in story telling, and classes in all parts of the art of drama.

Three
Georgia's Crowning Beauty: 1923

Frank Troutman and Miss Gladys Slappey (pictured on page 46) were elected king and queen in 1923. The election this year was different than the year before. The general population nominated their candidates, and the festival committee members then voted secretly on those nominations. In response to their being given such a high honor, Mr. Troutman and Miss Slappey wrote the following in the local paper, "Reversing the ancient order of things (of Kings), we promise to be your faithful and loyal subjects, ready to serve you, whenever you can use us—for you know—No spot on earth is more cherished by each than this 'Garden of Eden,' our 'County of Peach.' signed Frank—of the House of Troutman and Gladys—of the House of Slappey."

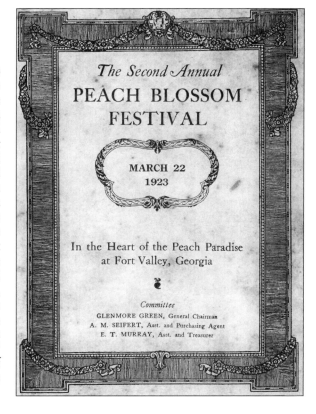

The 1923 festival was greatly anticipated by the people of Fort Valley and others who had either been at the first affair or had heard about it. It was expected that even more people would come, so nine committees were set up to cover all the needs. In addition, a table attendant committee of sixty-four women was formed to help take care of two sections of tables each at the barbecue. It was well needed as it was estimated that twenty-five thousand people attended the festival.

The American Legion volunteered to help the civil authorities with parking cars, directing people and traffic, and in keeping general public order. No one was allowed to sell anything during the festival. Any commercialism was prohibited for the day. It was said that everyone from everywhere would be welcome, except crooks. But if they came, arrangements would be made for them, too.

The date for the festival was only set two weeks ahead of time. It was very important that the peach blossoms were at their peak. Imagine the organization that it took to be ready for such a large event in that short amount of time. Also, in preparation for the festival, hundreds of costumes had to be made for the pageant and tables made for the barbecue and food secured. In accordance with cleaning up the town and making everything look nice and neat, the mayor had every tree, telegraph pole, telephone pole, and every electric light pole in the city limits white-washed to the height of 6.5 feet.

New streets were cut to make getting around easier for guests. New water faucets were placed around town. To help with the large crowd wanting to view the pageant, seats were built with several thousand feet of lumber. Everything seemed to be in place, but three days before the festival, a freeze hit and there was also a heavy rain for a week. Despite the bad weather prior to the event, on that Thursday the sun came out, and it turned into a beautiful day.

In this year's festival, there was a concert by the United States Army 29th Infantry Band downtown. Then, an automobile tour could be taken through the orchards to view the blooms. For the first time a parade was held, featuring industrial floats and decorated automobiles. Some of the floats were sponsored by the Atlanta Chamber of Commerce, Twin Oaks Fruit Farm, Fort Valley Lumber Company, Montezuma and Macon Kiwanis Clubs, just to name a few.

After the barbecue was the long-awaited pageant, *Georgia's Crowning Glory*. It told the history of the state and recognized some of her famous sons and daughters. Of course, the real crowning glory of Georgia, at that point in time, was the heralded peach. It was estimated that the cost of the entire festival for 1923 was $15,000.

The barbecue was even greater than the year before. Ten thousand and forty feet of pit were dug for the occasion, and 20,000 pounds of meat were served; thus ended the lives of 204 hogs. There were two hundred people that helped with the feast alone. There were 700 gallons of Brunswick stew and 3,000 loaves of bread. The tables to serve the food, end to end, were 1.75 miles long. Therefore, the servers had 3 miles of room to accommodate the crowds. There were also 1,000 gallons of coffee, served from large city sprinkler trucks that had been sanitized.

Mrs. F.W. Withoft wrote the poem, "Georgia's Crowning Glory—A Pageant of Peachland." Here, Mrs. Ashby McCord represented the "Spirit of Georgia." She wore a costume that was comprised of the colors of the state flag.

The pageant was a procession of famous people and groups who had a great influence in Georgia history. However, Mrs. Withoft did include a section on industry and agriculture in the state. Hence, there were Georgia flowers, birds, trees, butterflies, fruits, vegetables, crops, nuts, and even pests. The highlight, of course, was the Georgia peach. A group of ladies represented the peach trees and danced in celebration of its greatness.

Miss Margaret Jones (pictured at the top of the page) played one of the estimated fifty peach tree characters. There were also little peach blossoms which could not be overlooked.

To gain the perspective of the enormity of the pageant itself, one must know that there were seven hundred actors involved. In addition, there was a chorus of seventy-five, who sang much of the story being told and an orchestra that provided the music. The pageant began with the

coronation of King Troutman and Queen Slappey. Next, the Spirit of Georgia appeared and summoned her three gifts—History, Industry, and Agriculture—and presented them to the king and queen. The procession then began.

Here was the Spirit of Georgia in her litter and one of the nubian slaves who carried her to the king and queen. In the background are the soldiers of World War I.

Oglethorpe and his men claimed Georgia as their own in 1733. Oglethorpe was played here by C.E. Martin.

Representing Georgia's era of English rule were Continental soldiers. Some of the participants were Chester Wilson, Bass Vinson, Edgar Murray, Mr. Austin, Mr. Steed, J.E. Bledsoe, Thomas Cheek, and Robert Tuggle.

A large part of the beginning of Georgia's history was about the Native Americans. The chief was played by Dave C. Strother, a well-known farmer and collector of many different varieties of camellias. His camellia gardens became the National Headquarters of the American Camellia Society. One of the famous Native Americans was Tomochichi, who was played by Ben Fincher. Tomochichi made important treaties with Oglethorpe, the founder of Georgia, concerning Georgia land.

With the soldiers of the American Revolution were the color bearer, played by Lynn Brown, and the drummer boy, played by Will Tharpe. In this picture were some of the colonial children, ladies, and gentlemen. The children were: Cornelia Brown, Lottie Norton, Robert Tharpe, Ruth McMillian, Mary Evans, and Leighton Shepard Jr.

The veterans of the War Between the States were always highly honored and revered. Some of the men were: M.A. Edwards, W.G. Jordan, Mr. Doles, Mr. Cliett, J.T. Aultman, K.J. Carpenter, N.C. Rutherford, Mr. Hunter, and Mr. Quitman.

These women are students from Wesleyan, the first women's college in America, which was founded in 1836 at Macon, just a few miles north of Fort Valley. These ladies carried the school banner in the telling of the history of Georgia. They were Viloula White, Miss Mildred Anderson, Miss Maymsie Ousley, and Miss Pauline Carter, all of Fort Valley.

In addition were Miss Kathryn Pate of Albany, Miss Celeste Copeland of Greensboro, Miss Elizabeth McRae of Mount Vernon, Miss Lucile Berry of East Point, Miss Martha Few of Madison, and Miss Bessie Darsey of Bainbridge.

The Old South was featured with her veterans and her "people," meaning servants and slaves. During many of the entrances by groups, the orchestra played or the chorus sang special

selections. When the Old South group appeared the chorus sang "Sing Me A Song of the Sunny South." They also performed a medley of old songs.

Among the famous Georgians were these four men: Sidney Lanier, played by George Culpepper Jr.; Joel Chandler Harris, played by O.M. Houser; Dr. Crawford W. Long, played by W. Lee Houser; and Ty Cobb, played by Paul Murray.

Here are a few of the butterflies and other creatures that had a role in the pageant. How creative the ladies must have been to think of costumes for asparagus, radishes, tobacco, and the pecan, among others. It is of interest that the pests that were recognized were the currulio, boll weevil, spotted lady bug, pecan borer, click beetle, peach tree borer, devil's riding horse, grasshopper, locust, and soldier bug.

Four
Peach of the World: 1924

For the third festival, Mrs. Alfred Hume (Helen), was elected queen. Elbert M. Whiting was elected king. Mr. Whiting was a banker and local businessman. Both are pictured together on page 62.

The 1924 festival appears to be the most popular and well documented of the five fetes. More photographs survived from this year than from any other.

With every year the festivals grew, and the task of even planning the affair became overwhelming. In 1923, there were nine committees to handle the details. In 1924, there were seventeen in place. The general manager of the festival was Col. Charles Leighton Shepard. The Kiwanis Club in Fort Valley sponsored the event. E.T. Murray was president.

Third Annual Peach Blossom Festival

C. L. SHEPARD, GENERAL CHAIRMAN

Fort Valley, Georgia

March 27, 1924

Program

9:00 A. M.—Concerts, Al-Sihah Shrine Band. *Fincher Park.*
Central R. R. Shop Band. *Railroad Station.*

9:30 A. M.—Parade of Floats and Decorated Automobiles.

10:00 A. M.—Exhibition Flights—U. S. Army Airplanes. *Interest Citizens Military Training Camps.*

10:30 A. M.—Music, Features, Street Exhibits, Thrills.

11:00 A. M.—Address, Reminiscences of Military Service, Maj. General David C. Shanks, Commander Fourth Corps Area U. S. A.

11:30 A. M.—Music, 29th Infantry Band. Al-Sihah Shrine Band. Central R. R. Shop Band.

12:00 M. —Old Fashoined Georgia Barbecue.

1:30 P. M.—PAGEANT, "Peach of The World." *Oakland Heights.*
Music by 29th Infantry Band.

Over one hundred policemen from all over middle Georgia were called in to help with controlling the crowds. Also giving assistance to the American Legion were the Boy Scouts. The estimates of how many people actually attended the festival ranged from thirty-five thousand to fifty thousand. Each year the festival committee added new events. There were three bands that played. Airplanes came from Montgomery, Alabama, for exhibitions. The parade grew larger, with over thirty floats and decorated automobiles. Much emphasis was on the military, and many dignitaries from all over the state were invited. Prominent businessmen from all over the country came to this now nationally known event.

The barbecue had also grown in size. Now there were 2 acres, fenced by barbed wire, which held the pits for the "cue." The year before, people took sides of meat off the pits and absconded with them. This year the pits were guarded, and at night the gates to the pits were chain locked. Next to the pits were 10 fenced-off acres, which held the tables for serving the meal. There were as many as thirty-seven gates through which people could enter. At each entrance, there was a table built in three decks. Each table held 1,500 plates of barbecue.

The pageant was again written by Mrs. Mabel Swartz Withoft. It was called, *Peach of the World*. This wonderful work told the history of the peach, from its beginnings in China to the present time. Again, seven hundred participants acted out the story. Magnificent costumes were made to represent the countries that had a connection with the peach. Thirty-five peach states were also depicted. The total time to perform the pageant was two hours and twenty minutes.

Each pageant had been directed by Miss Pauline Eaton Oak. She was from Maine and worked with the National Community Services organization, which encouraged such cultural events. She spent many hours in Fort Valley working with the community on how to present such a grand-scaled production. Her talent and skill seemed to meet each challenge. It was said that the staging and set production of this pageant was truly amazing.

Queen Helen Crandell Hume had the credentials for royalty, as she was a member of the Colonial Dames and Mayflower Society. Her beautiful robe was worn by the very famous silent screen star, Mary Pickford, in the movie *Dorothy Vernon of Haddon Hall*.

The king and queen entered the stage area on a large decorated float. Six black horses, provided by American Express, pulled the royalty to where they were to be officially crowned. The archbishop who would do the honor was played by Rev. Loy Warwick, pastor of the local Methodist church.

A special stage was built to hold the king and queen, their courtiers, ladies, pages, flower girls, heralds, and lone jester. From there they viewed the pageant. For the first time, tickets were sold for this part of the festival. Ten thousand seats were made available.

The main speaker for the day was Major-General David C. Shanks (shown to the left), who was the commander of the Fourth Corps at Fort McPherson, Georgia. He was one of the honorary pallbearers at the funeral of President Harding. Commander Shanks, who was soon to retire, had already received the Distinguished Service Medal from the Army and from the Navy.

Fort Valley had a very popular float for the parade. It represented Fort Valley as the hub of the peach tree industry with over sixteen million peach trees planted in a 100-mile radius of the town. In the center was Miss Elizabeth Everett, who had been elected as "Miss Fort Valley." She was the daughter of Jim Everett, who was mentioned earlier in the book as the "King of the Barbecue." From the center of the hub, pink spokes led to ladies who represented different cities and towns connected with the peach industry.

The parade this year had been expanded and had many more entries than the year before. For the first time the floats and decorated automobiles were judged by a panel of three men, two from New York and one from Philadelphia. The first place winner was the float from Montezuma, a small town southwest of Fort Valley. The float was sponsored by the Montezuma City Council. They received $75 in prize money. Miss Louise Hays was Miss Montezuma. Other ladies seated in the pink shell were Misses Frances Felton, Virginia DeVaughn, Ruth Haugabook, and Clarabelle Maffet.

The second place winner was Randolph County, which is in southwest Georgia. Its theme was "Randolph County Diversifies." Its sponsors were awarded $50.

The third place winner was from Monticello, a town north of Macon. The prize awarded was $25 dollars. The parade was delayed for some time while the crowd waited for the governor to arrive by train from Atlanta.

Honorable mention was given to one of the two floats entered by the Central of Georgia Railroad. It depicted a Pullman coach full of children.

This decorated car was from Roberta, just a short distance from Fort Valley. Note that even the wheels and spokes of the car were decorated with paper.

The Atlanta Chamber of Commerce's car was very nicely decorated with blossoms and was led by a butterfly. In the car were Miss Erskine Jarnigan and Miss Louise Barnwell. Also in the car were Mayor Walter A. Sims and B.S. Barker, secretary of the chamber.

The Fort Valley Crate and Lumber Company had "peaches" in crates made by the business.

The City of Macon fully supported the festival in many ways. For their entry into the parade, the Retail Merchant's Bureau sponsored a float that highlighted Miss Macon and her attendants. The person chosen as Miss Macon was Miss Marion Elliott.

Six pits, 600 feet long, were dug for the cooking of the four hundred hogs used for the barbecue. For two full days the process continued, with the help of six hundred men. To help keep it fresh until it could be cooked, the meat was kept iced down in two refrigerated train cars. Fifty thousand pounds of barbecue were served.

The preparation of every item on the menu was massive. Here one can see that the coffee is being made. Consider, however, the making of the Brunswick stew, which took two cases of celery, four barrels of vinegar, 600 pounds of salt, 60 gallons of canned corn, 80 gallons of tomatoes, 60 gallons of tomato sauce, 18 gallons of English peas, 50 pounds of onions, and 20 bushels of potatoes.

Peach of the World tells the history of the peach. The pageant began with the arrival of Pomona, the Goddess of Fruit. At her arrival seeds, blossoms, and fruit dance in celebration of her coming. Here are some of those dancers.

The peach had an extensive history in Japan, India, Persia, and Greece. Miss Audrey Fagan played a Persian maiden. Note all the detail on the handmade costume.

Pomona then summoned onto the stage the Past, the Present, and the Future. The Past, played by Mrs. J.W. Rundell, told the story of the peach in times long ago. The beginning of the peach was in China. In this episode, Miss Myrtice Patterson represented a Chinese bride.

According to the story, the peach was in Persia around 330 B.C. In the above photograph are Persian dancers and maids. Some of the characters were played by Charlie Mathews, Helen Marshall, George B. Culpepper, Emily Anderson, Annie Shepard, Havilyn Nance, and Hugh Anderson.

The peach then spread to the continent of Europe, to Italy and France. In France, monks grew the peach. In the countries of England, Belgium, Holland, and Spain, they saw the widespread popularity of the fruit grow. Here Martha Whiting represented Belgium in a wedding dress from England. The dress belonged to Mrs. Claude DuPree. Miss Whiting was sister to the king of the 1924 festival.

From Europe, the peach found its way to Mexico. Here, Miss Louise English stands with her pages, Clifford Holmes Prator and Frederick Solomon.

After the Past told her story, the Present summoned America and its states. The Present was played by Miss Ruth Houser. America came to call on the peach-growing states. Miss America was Mrs. John Allen, and her page was Frank Miller Neil.

One of the states represented in the pageant was New Jersey, played by Miss Christine Evans, daughter of A.J. Evans ("The Peach King"). Kneeling before Miss Evans were her pages Mildred Kendrick and Ruth Howard McMillan.

There were thirty-five states summoned, as these were the states where the peach was commercially grown. Each state was dressed in the state colors and carried the state flowers. There were two pages assigned to each state, and one would carry a banner with the state name. California, played by Mrs. W.S. White, is shown here with two pages, played by Coleman Nichols and Dodderidge Houser.

On the lawn of peach grower J.H. Hale's home, the ladies who represented the countries and the states in the pageant pose in costume for a photograph. Pictured in front of these women are

the children who accompanied them across the stage.

Anticipation mounted as Georgia entered the stage to honor the peach. The commercial peach industry had been born in the heart of middle Georgia, and this industry was a great gift to the world. Georgia, played by Miss Thelma Wilson, the first festival's queen is pictured here with her pages: Harris Dyes and Charles Culpepper.

Never before had the ladies of Fort Valley and the surrounding area been highlighted as they were during the five festivals. These ladies were just a few of the hundreds that were able to participate in the pageants. However, there were hundreds more who made costumes, banners for the streets, helped cook the food and serve it, handed out flyers or tags to visitors, kept guests in their homes, or had other duties. They were all volunteers.

These ladies were part of the cast of *Girls in Pink* and carried peach blossoms. The director of the pageant, Miss Pauline Oak, used all ages in as many ways possible during every part of the fete. For the final part of the story, the character Future, played by Miss Mary Belle Houser, revealed a sea of blossoms to the world.

These women played some of the leading roles in the pageant. Among them were: Miss Gladys Slappey, Mrs. J.W. Rundell, Miss Ruth Houser, Miss Mary Belle Houser, Miss Wilma Orr, Miss Helen Marshall, Miss Audrey Fagan, Mrs. Robert Marchman, Mrs. John Allen,

Miss Thelma Wilson, Miss Elizabeth Everett, and, of course, pages Mildred Kendrick and Ruth Howard McMillan.

The butterflies came out with the peach blossoms and the girls in pink, and everyone danced. The bands then played "America the Beautiful," as all seven hundred cast members and the ten thousand spectators sang. What a moment it must have been.

This little butterfly was Miss Mary McCoy. Even the smallest got to play a part in this grand affair. As the festival ended and people found their way back to the corners of the world, the festival was proclaimed as the best one yet. However, there was now concern over whether the festival had gotten too big for such a small town. Still, there were few problems and the plans for festival number four were already in the minds of many.

Five
The Trail of Pink Pedals: 1925

For the first time, the peach blossom festival was made into a two-day event. The year before there had been some question about whether the mere size of the crowds could be handled as the festival grew. In 1925, the festival committee decided to hold the fete on two days and just repeat the program. They expanded the hours of the activities and added an evening performance by the Sixth Calvary riding team. Added to the night events was a pyrotechnic display.

PROGRAM

Fourth Annual Peach Blossom Festival
Fort Valley, Georgia
March 19th and 20th, 1925

(*Each day's Program complete within itself*)
Thursday's Program will be repeated Friday

Coronation Ceremonies	9:45 A. M.
Float Parade	10:15 A. M.
Exhibition Drills and Fancy Riding—Detachment Sixth Cavalry U. S. Army	11:15 A. M.
Old Fashioned Georgia Barbecue	12:15 P. M.
Pageant: "The Trail of Pink Petals"	2:00 P. M.
Exhibition Drills; Cossack Riding; Roman Riding; High Jumping; Night Attack, Star Shells and Pyrotechnics—Detachment Sixth Cavalry U. S. Army	8:00 P. M.

Mr. Samuel Mathews and Miss Ruth Evans were elected king and queen for the 1925 festival. Here they stand in the front of the home of her parents, Mr. and Mrs. A.J. Evans.

This year the planners went ahead and set the dates for the festival by February. All nineteen committees for the fete were well at work on their assignments by this time. Even the dancers for the pageant were rehearsing.

orgeous Pageant in Honor of the Georgia Peac

Thousands of Visitors Heard Pageant Through W. E. Public Address System

In the grandstand, the king and queen (pictured above) watched the pageant with their court and thousands of others.

The festival had grown in national recognition over the last three years. Hollywood was getting involved by sending movie crews to film the festival for the theater news reels. Pathe, Graphic, Fox, and Kinogram studios were all present for the fete. *National Geographic* sent Jacob Gayer, one of their photographers, to cover the festival. In 1926, the magazine included the Fort Valley event in an article about Georgia.

Miss Oak and Mrs. Withoft teamed up again to present the pageant honoring the peach. The pageant had become what one reporter called the "heart and soul" of the festival. Forty acres of land had been secured for festival activities, 11 acres were to be used for parking, and an amphitheater was built on 4 acres. Twenty-eight thousand and nine hundred tickets were printed to be sold for the pageant. The charge would be $1 a ticket.

Every year more money and more time was being put into the festivals. How long could this go on before this little town would become exhausted of energy and resources? Already they were having to do two programs to handle the crowds. Would selling tickets to events now reduce the number of attendants? It was becoming evident that some big decisions were going to have to be made in the near future.

The coronation of the king and queen occurred at the beginning of the day. A throne and stage were set up downtown in Fincher Park, underneath the water tower. "Cardinal" David Howard, pastor of the Baptist church, crowned the couple, who were attended by four pages. The small children carried the crowns, scepter, and the signet ring. One of the pages accidentally dropped

the ring as he ascended the platform. Fortunately, a reporter found it in time for the ceremony to continue without interruption. A carriage brought the court ladies, flower girls, and pages to the throne area. After the coronation was complete, nine courtiers arrived on horseback, carrying banners in purple and gold. They, too, joined the others alongside the king and queen.

The procession to the throne began at the home of A.J. Evans. The costumes were designed after the fashion of the Louis XV period. The dress for the queen was made of gold cloth with gold tulle ruffles, and rhinestones, gold beads, and pearls accented the collar and bodice. The queen also wore gold slippers. The train to the gown was purple silk and lined in white ermine. Miss Ruth Evans designed and made the dress with the help of Mrs. A.J. Evans, Mrs. J.D. Kendrick, and Miss Electra Weeks.

The newspapers reported Queen Ruth's grueling morning schedule before the festival. She had to arise at 7:30, "too early for a queen." She would breakfast with her parents and then retire to her boudoir to be dressed. Her toilet would be overseen by her mother. At 9:00 the carriage would arrive and the processional to the throne would begin.

For the first time, people were charged for the barbecue lunch. It was 50¢ a plate. It was reported that 45,000 paper cups and 62,000 paper plates were used. About 40,000 pounds of barbecue were served. It took two hundred cords of wood to cook the three hundred pigs. There were no consistent reports of the total number of people attending the festival for both days. Some suggested there were up to sixty thousand people.

There were thirty-six floats in the parade. The winner, again, was Montezuma. Their float centered around a fountain done in white and pink. They won $100 in prize money.

The Central of Georgia Railroad won second place with its observation-sleeping coach, designed after cars that passed through Fort Valley. The car was covered with white blossoms and pink buds. Seven children from Fort Valley rode in the train car. They were Evelyn Evans, Anzie Newton, Ruth Brown, Julia McAfee, Virginia McMichael, Geraldine Crawford, and Jule Lambert. The children even had costumes made for them by the Miller Decorating Company of Oklahoma City.

Thomaston, a farming town about 40 miles northwest of Fort Valley, won third place in the contest. It was reported that the float did not win for beauty but for cleverness.

Fort Valley, in 1924, had "seceded" from Houston County by starting the new county of Peach. Although there was much controversy regarding this action, Houston County made a good will gesture by entering a float. This ship of maidens was sure to meet with approval by the crowd.

One of the decorated cars in the parade was used to advertise a car company. It is unknown where the company was from. Note the draped windows in the background and the flags on the car and along the street.

The float that obtained honorable mention was the City of Albany, south of Fort Valley. Albany's "peach" was the pecan. Therefore, they came proclaiming the fame for their pecans.

They used russet and gold as their colors, instead of the white and pinks that so many used.

Americus was a bustling town south of Fort Valley. Here they centered their float on a farmer

with his plow and young maidens with peach blossoms.

From Perry, just 12 miles south of town, came this decorated truck advertising Thurmond Grey watermelons.

This float from Macon was beautifully done. It highlighted the queen of Macon coming out of a bloom. It also had her throne in the back, decorated with many blossoms. The house in the background was owned by H.C. Harris, one time owner of the Harris House Hotel, later the Winona Hotel.

The pageant for 1925 was called *Trail of Pink Petals* and was written by Mrs. Withoft and directed by Pauline Oak. Miss Oak always did a great deal of research before directing the story at the festival. She had done other pageant work in Washington, D.C., and in Florida. She also had performed in small theaters. She graduated from Leland Powers School of the Spoken Word in Boston. She was also employed by the Kentucky College for Women, where she taught expression.

The history of the peach was told very much like it was in the pageant of the previous year. The scenes took place at Mount Olympus, where Pomona, the Goddess of Fruit, called on her five favorite fruits to come dance for her. In this picture the grape had come to please her.

The five fruits called on by Pomona were the madcap grape, winsome cherry, dainty orange, sprightly apple, and the radiant peach. It was the peach that won the goddess' heart. Played by Miss Charlie Mathews, the peach was the center figure for the rest of the pageant. She did four solos and two duet dances. She later told reporters that she had never taken dancing lessons and that she had made up most of what she did.

The peach traveled to China and on around the world to the different countries where she was planted and then grew, to the great delight of the citizens of that part of the world. Miss Margaret Whiting was one of the one hundred Chinese maidens that celebrated the peach.

The peach made her way to America and to Georgia where she met Fort Valley, played by Arthur Vinson. A wedding was held and the match was made. The maid of honor was Miss Frances Holland. The best man was Samuel Henry Rumph, founder of the peach industry in Georgia. The minister was Judge M.C. Mosely.

These children attended the wedding and no doubt danced with the other one thousand who had a part in the pageant. The 29th Infantry Band from Fort Benning, Georgia, furnished the music. Note the mountain in the background. Over 2 acres of pine saplings were cut for the trees in the scenery. In addition to all the day's activities, crop-dusting planes flew overhead to spread peach petals over the crowd.

At the wedding of the peach and Fort Valley were twenty bridesmaids, who represented the twenty peach-growing counties in Georgia. Shown here are America and some of her states.

America was played by Mrs. Leighton Shepard, wife of C.L. Shepard who was the general chairman of the festival.

This was one of the thousands of peach tags that were given away to advertise the peach blossom festival. They were also given as souvenirs to the people who came to the festivities.

Six
The Prodigal Peach: 1926

The final Peach Blossom Festival was held in 1926. Although the fetes had been more than successful, the size and the cost were becoming unbearable. Changes had to be made if the festivals were to continue. In January of 1926, the general chairman of the festival, Ralph Newton, asked for other communities and organizations around the state to help with this year's event. It was stated that the fete "could no longer be considered a local affair, but a project in which the entire state should be allowed to cooperate."

Mr. John Allen and his wife Arline (pictured below) were the chosen king and queen for the 1926 festival. Allen was one of the largest peach growers in the middle Georgia area, with 2,500 acres. He had sixty thousand peach-bearing trees alone. The Allens lived on the old Allen homestead called "Twin Oaks." The couple was very popular and very well known for the grand barbecues held on their plantation.

The dates for the festival were set for March 11 and 12. There was no time to lose in getting people and communities involved. The Macon and Atlanta Chambers of Commerce underwrote thousands of tickets for the pageant. Marshalville and Montezuma were each given an episode to perform in the story and supplied their own costumes as well. People from all over the state and many from other states were chosen to make up the king and queen's court. The festival was now to be a Georgian affair.

The festival committee bought 40 acres of land to be known as the pageant grounds. An amphitheater with fourteen thousands seats was built, and a loudspeaker system for the stage and seating areas was also purchased.

The costume of Queen Aline was designed in the Louis XV period. The colors of lavender, purple, and gold were used. The gown was lavender satin, with panels of beads. The robe had a collar of gold, and the ensemble was accented with rhinestones. She wore satin slippers. Miss Lucy Finney, who designed all the costumes for the first festival, also designed the costumes for the king and queen in this festival.

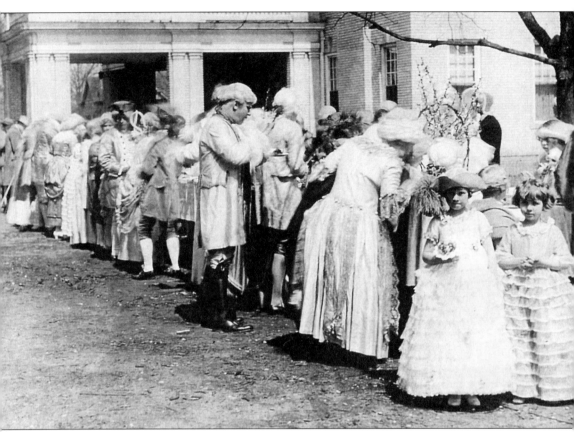

The first day of the festival was canceled due to rain. The success of the entire event now rested on one day. The weather smiled on the small town, for it turned out very pleasant. Near downtown, at one of the beautiful grand homes, a lunch was prepared for the royal court, before the coronation ceremonies.

After lunch, the soon to be king and queen were taken in a carriage, designed in the Louis XV style, to the pageant grounds by six black horses supplied by American Express. The harnesses were gold and ornate in style, and the horses were adorned with plumes of purple and gold. The costumes of the royal court also followed the Louis XV style.

The parade was longer, with more entries, and the pageant was even grander than the year before. Fifteen hundred people were cast in parts. So many children were used that holidays from school were declared by Fort Valley and surrounding communities. Special trains were arranged to bring folks from Atlanta, Macon, and other Georgia cities.

Fort Valley prepared for the onslaught of visitors. They had invited the world to their paradise and the world had attended. The Peach Blossom Festival was so well known that it was even referred to in the popular cartoon, The Gumps. Mr. Gump said that it took an apple to get

man kicked out of paradise, but it is a peach that will get him back in. Unfortunately, paradise was about to close its doors.

The parades were very popular. It was thought forty thousand people attended the last festival and crowded the streets of Fort Valley. The Byron float won third place in the float competition. Note the people sitting on the roof of the building across the street with their feet hanging over the side. The water tower that had been so prominent in the landscape of the other festivals, here at Fincher Park, was removed to improve the view.

The crowd gathered for the parade. Note the Macon YWCA First Aid Station in the background. One wonders where each person came from and why they were there. Was it for

the parade, barbecue, or pageant? Was it their first visit? What did they think of all the sights, sounds, and smells that must have existed for such a large affair?

One of the bands in town to entertain the crowds was the Technological High School from Atlanta. The other band called upon to play was The Central of Georgia Railroad band, called The Right of Way. Note the floats in the background.

Of all the floats that entered the parade, Albany and Newnan tied for first place. Talbotton was third in the competition. Talbotton's entry had a fair maiden sitting on a quarter moon. Her love was at her feet, with cupid shooting an arrow at his heart.

Twenty thousand pounds of barbecue were prepared this year. The meat for the "cue" was purchased from Swift and Company of Moultrie. It was brought to Fort Valley in a special refrigerated car. The meat was then taken directly off the car as it was needed.

This picture shows how the picnic grounds were set up. In the background is the back of the stage for the pageant. To cut the five thousand loaves of bread needed for the lunch, an electrical machine was used for the first time. Still, it took over twenty-four hours to slice all the bread.

The royal couple arrived at the throne by carriage. The background was a large fan made of the colors of the rainbow, and the throne was colored gold. John Farren of Macon designed the set, as well as the carriage. The cardinal was played by Rev. Loy Warwick, who had performed at several festivals. The ladies and gentlemen of the court surrounded the couple during the moment for which they had long awaited.

The king had his suit made of lavender satin, with a gold brocaded vest and a gold jacket. He also wore knee breeches with silk hose. The jester between the king and queen was John S. Rumph of Marshallville. The Allens gave a ball at their home for the members of the court that evening.

The pageant for 1926 was called *The Prodigal Peach*, again written by Mrs. Withoft. It had six episodes, with Mount Olympus being the center stage for each part of the story. The narrator of the story was the Spirit of Pageantry, played by Mrs. H.P. Sanchez. Again Pomona, the Goddess of Fruit, was one of the main characters. She asked her sister, Earth, to create a new fruit for her. Of course, Earth produced the peach, and the tale of adventure around the world began. A globe was built as part of the scenery. It was constructed by Cornelius Hall at his shop. The world measured 7 feet in diameter and was made of wire topped by cement. When Mr. Hall finished his creation, he was unable to get it out the shop door. Not to be outdone, a side of the building was torn off, and the earth was carried out to its new home at Mount Olympus.

The scene in this photograph showed the birth of the little peach. The Baby Peach was played by Helen Forsyth Harris, daughter of Mr. and Mrs. Saunders Harris. She was the youngest to dance in a peach pageant.

Earth was played by Miss Christine Evans, daughter of A.J. Evans and sister to the 1925 queen, Ruth Evans. Every member of the cast had to pay for their own costume. It was reported that some of the costumes averaged around $500.

The Maiden Peach was played by Miss Dorothy Hale, a talented dancer and a native of Fort Valley. She studied in New York and performed in several Southern states.

The gods and goddesses of mythology were called to join Pomona, Earth, and the Spirit of Pageantry in the telling of the story of the prodigal Peach leaving her home to travel the world. One of the gods was Bacchus, played by Jonas Hillyer. Other gods were Jupiter, Juno, Mercury, Apollo, Mars, Athena, Diana, and Venus.

The Peach traveled first to Asia, where all the counties came to pay her homage. They built her a temple where she could reside. Asia was played by J.S. Croxton, and the main dancer for the episode was Mrs. Jack Reed.

All the main countries of Asia (India, China, Japan, and Persia) were represented. The entire cast of two hundred were from the town of Montezuma. There were two camels used for this episode, on loan from the Spark's Circus.

Because of pests that attacked, the Peach fled to Europe. Here she found a new home with the help of England, Holland, France, and Belgium. The town of Marshallville provided the cast of one hundred for this episode. Europe was played by Samuel Rumph.

The Spanish dancers that performed were Miss Charlie Mathews and Cornelius Hall, who built the world on Mount Olympus. Miss Mathews had been the star of the 1925 festival, in her role as the dancing peach. She played two parts in the 1926 pageant. She was one of Earth's attendants and then played a Spanish dancer.

Pests again chased the Peach away, and she traveled to America and finally to Georgia, where she was united with Science to overcome her many enemies of nature. There she was wed to Science, played by Dave Strother.

After the ceremony, four hundred women appeared, all wearing pink. They held peach blossoms and formed a beautiful orchard. Pomona sadly left to go back to her world, for she knew that the Peach had found her final home in the state of Georgia. At times during the pageant, there were as many as five hundred actors on stage. The entire play was heard over Atlanta's WSB Radio by thousands of listeners.

One of the many props for the stage included a ship on which the Peach traveled to America. Over 2,000 feet of lumber and 2,000 feet of beaver board were used to make the scenery. One of the larger pieces for the set was a ship made in the likeness of the Mayflower and the

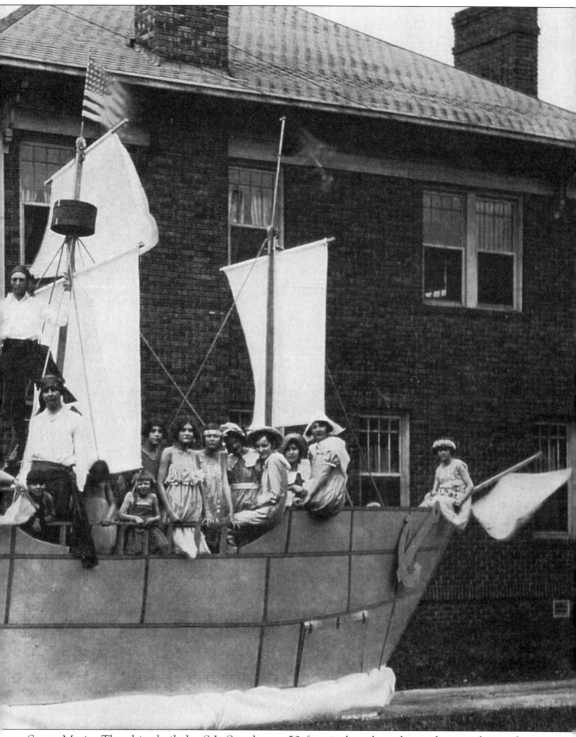

Santa Maria. The ship, built by S.J. Steed, was 50 feet in length and was decorated in red, white, and blue.

This is a photograph of Mrs. Etta Carithers Houston, the originator of the Peach Blossom Festival.

Afterword

Unsuspectingly, the crowd on Friday, March 12, had just walked away from the last pageant and the last Peach Blossom Festival. It had been a glorious display of creativity and salesmanship, all of of which had come from one woman's idea about a small town putting on a festival to honor an agricultural crop. To Mrs. Etta Carithers Houston, the originator of the idea; to Mrs. Mabel Swartz Withoft, author of all the wonderful pageants; to Miss Pauline Eaton Oak, who directed each pageant with enthusiasm, love, and great creativity, I dedicate this book. Without them, the World's Peach Paradise, in our imagination, would not have existed.

This area was rightly called a paradise for the peach because it was true in that there were at least sixteen million peach trees planted in the middle Georgia area. More peaches were shipped from there than from any other place in the world. The people and peach growers wanted to show the world the peach industry and how great it was to be connected to the peach. So, the Peach Blossom Festival was born.

In the five years of festivals, Fort Valley shared the beauty of the peach, the generosity of her people, and the creativity of her minds. The townsfolk opened the doors to their homes, hearts, and pocketbooks. They gave of their time and their resources. The festivals truly were a town affair. It was estimated that fully eighty percent of the population of Fort Valley, both black and white, participated in some way in the fetes.

But the bright vision of having annual festivals "as long as there are peach blossoms" was soon to be overshadowed by the size and cost of such an undertaking. The organizers, in some ways, had created a beast of a beauty. By the third festival, there were signs that they were over their heads. However, they were not going to give up on having the best festival possible. By 1926, the fete cost an estimated $50,000. Over the course of the five festivals over one hundred eighty-five thousand people had attended and partaken of Fort Valley's fruit.

To be bigger and better, there were charges for the barbecue and pageant. The rest of the state of Georgia was increasingly asked to participate and to take on some of the expense. Land was purchased and money spent on large scenery, loudspeaker systems, and an amphitheater. Costumes were elaborate and costly, even when the actors paid for the outfits themselves. However, the largest sign of possible collapse came when Pauline Oak wrote a letter to the people of Fort Valley in February of 1926. It was a heartfelt appeal for help and for self-evaluation. She wrote, "Are you finding joy in what you have elected to do . . .Have we lost the precious spirit of childhood . . . You expect so much of me that I grow frightened sometimes at the mere thought of it, you must realize that I cannot meet those expectations unless you do your part." The spirit of the people of Fort Valley was showing signs of wear.

On the commercial front, the peach industry was on the verge of collapse. There had been too many that thought they could make themselves rich from those luscious peaches. More and more states were planting the fruit. The market "went bust" in 1926 and 1927. The interest in peaches and festivals was over. The idea of a festival was seldom discussed again. Fort Valley tried to have a county fair instead, but with little success.

The dreams of many had been fulfilled in one special day of fairy tales on fancy floats or old Southern barbecues fit for a king and queen. They imagined the adventures of mythological characters in the form of gods and goddesses and fruits and watched the stories acted out before their very eyes. But, now it was over.

For years to come, the remains of Mount Olympus and the amphitheater would stand as reminders to those who passed by, that when a town pulls together great things can be accomplished. More importantly, the relics stood for visions and dreams of a group of people that were larger than life itself. For five years they made a small, unknown, rural community "The World's Peach Paradise."